CANDLE MAGIC
FOR BEGINNERS

*A Simple Guide to Wiccan Candle
Magic for Spells, Rituals, Love,
Protection, and Prosperity*

TABLE OF CONTENTS

INTRODUCTION

*"Look at how a single candle can
both defy and define the darkness."*
– Anne Frank.

Anne Frank's words carry more truth to them than most people could imagine. We use candles to cast light when it's dark to see and find our way. Yet, despite this happening on the physical plane, candles can also be used to illuminate our spiritual plane. We all have darkness within us and surrounding us, but not in the physical sense. Anger, frustration, sadness, hate, jealousy, anxiety, and fear, that's the darkness within. The negative energy of some people you come in contact with and the horrible things that happen everywhere around us in the world that's the darkness surrounding us on emotional and spiritual levels. Candles can help you cast light and navigate your way through both.

For most people, candles are mere tools that we rarely use in our everyday lives. For witches, they are an integral part of their daily routine. The practice of using candle magick to bring about change in your life has been around for centuries. Many civilizations understood the power that a single candle holds and the changes it can manifest on the physical plane. Whether it's your fear of the future or years of suffering from low self-esteem, a candle can help you overcome that spiritual and emotional turmoil. It can help you shield yourself from that coworker's negative energy and the jealous relative's ill intentions toward you. A candle can help you heal from past traumas and grow emotionally, can help you find love, attract money and wealth, or even a job.

Candles can change your life, provided you have enough belief and understanding.

In this book, you will learn about the ancient practice of using candles to heal your pain -- physically, emotionally, and spiritually. You will learn to perform rituals and cast spells that can attract the things you want in life and banish those that no longer serve you. Every human out there has a list of wishes and dreams, as well as fears and pain. What few understand, however, is that you can control those things. You are in charge of your fate. You can banish the things holding you back and attract love, abundance, and happiness. With this book as your resource, you'll understand how you can do every one of those things.

I have spent many years researching and understanding these ancient witchcraft practices and its more modern movements, namely, Wicca. Contrary to popular beliefs, as a religion, Wicca aims to help people become happier versions of themselves. Witches promote a healthy lifestyle and a positive outlook on life. With the help of spells and rituals like the ones I will outline in this book, witches have managed to leverage the power of candles to bring about positive change into their lives. The spells I have curated in this book are carefully selected and curated to help anyone turn their life around. You don't have to be an experienced witch to perform the candle magick outlined here. If this is your first brush with these practices, you can still successfully get what you want if you follow my instructions.

I chose to write a book on this matter to help as many people harvest and utilize this ancient knowledge to simply become happier. I sought to put down my extensive expertise and insights into the world of spiritualism and Wicca in a simple, easy-to-use guide on candle magick, one of the most powerful tools at a witch's disposal, which can be read and practiced by anyone.

All you need is to keep an open mind and to be willing to try, and you'll learn everything you need to know about candle magick, starting with its origins and how each candle color means something, which you'll learn in the first chapter.

CHAPTER 1:

UNDERSTANDING CANDLE MAGIC

"The most tangible of all visible mysteries –– fire."
– Leigh Hunt.

Candle magic is a form of fire magic, and the importance of fire dates back to the earliest records we have of humans. As early as ancient man, humans have found a source of comfort and inspiration in the flames of a fire. It inspired awe and a sense of wonder in early men with its ability to keep them warm and cook food while also providing protection. To this very day, fire performs the same functions. Candles weren't around back then, but fires were used in ceremonial rituals like Samhain, where large bonfires were used to celebrate the occasion and commemorate the day.

The power of a flame to illuminate the darkness meant that when candles were invented, they had religious significance for many ancient civilizations. One of the oldest civilizations known to man, Ancient Egypt, had several gods and goddesses to whom homage was paid using candles. Followers of the goddess Isis placed candles all around her temples to be lit every hour of every day to symbolize constant light and hope. For pagans, it was Sabbat, which involved using candles with the Yule tree. For Wiccans, several ceremonies require the use of candles as a symbol of fire, one of the main elements from which witches draw power and energy. Even Christianity used candles on altars as part of the religion's rituals.

Candle Magic

Despite candle magick being associated with the fire element, it's actually more than that. Candle magick is alchemy for many witches – a combination of several elements. The candle flame is fire, the oxygen that feeds the flame is air, the wax that melts symbolizes water, and the wax that congeals is earth. Imbued with powerful and clear intentions, candle magick can then leverage the power of these four elements to attract the things you desire and banish what no longer serves you. It's also possible to add more elements to the candles you're using in your spells, like crystals (from the earth), herbs (also from the earth), and other components to make your spells more potent.

The great thing about candle magick, also known as sympathetic magic, is that it is simple in nature. For the most part, all you need is a candle. Yes, you need to charge the candle with your intention first, and you can make more intricate spells using other elements, but at the core of this kind of magick is a candle. Some scholars believe that successful candle magick consists of three elements: a clear intention in your head, visualizing your goal and the end result, and focusing on that intention until you can manifest the goal in real life.

Candles and Transformation in Wicca

Wicca is a modern practice of witchcraft, and it incorporates several ancient pagan practices dating back centuries ago. One practice uses candles for spells and as a means of divination or seeking insight and knowledge of the future. Why then do Wiccans and witches in general use magic, and why has fire been this important for many ancient civilizations? The importance of candle magic is how it uses fire to effect change and manifest desires. Fire is one of the most powerful elements in nature. It possesses the ability to destroy and transform, a beginning and an end of life. A fire can resemble the end of a forest, but it can also lay the foundation for an even more beautiful and greener one. Fire changes everything and anything it touches, a fearsome and powerful transformative power that can be used to transform your own life.

This transformative nature of fire is why it was held in high regard across different cultures and belief systems and why Wiccans harness its power through candle magick. By using candles in our rituals, we bring about change. We end the things that harm us and begin attracting what can help and please us. Wiccans believe that fire can connect us to our true selves, and in that connection lies the power to transform our fate and bring about positive change into our lives. I will show you how you can harness the power of the fire in candle rituals in the upcoming sections.

Candle Color Meaning

Not all candles are alike. Each color corresponds to a different intention, and if you want to make the most of your spell, you need to understand this color code and what each colored candle has the power to attract. Wiccans believe that burning a candle establishes a connection between the physical and spiritual realms using each candle's energy according to its color. It's this color energy that we tap into when we burn candles.

- **Green:** abundance, money, wealth, and fertility.
- **Red:** Courage, lust, love, strength, and sexuality.
- **Pink**: Friendship, love, kindness, and affecttion.
- **Orange**: Encouragement, attraction, support, and joy.
- **Dark Blue:** Emotional healing, change, adaptability, and psychic powers.
- **Gold:** Connection to the sun, professional success, and money.
- **Yellow:** Protection, divination, wisdom, mental prowess, prosperity, and persuasion.
- **Light Blue**: Patience, health, happiness, and compassion.

- **Brown:** Animal guidance, physical healing, and home.
- **Black:** Banishing negative energies and forces, healing, and psychic protection.
- **Purple:** Power, ambition, female confidence, and stress relief.
- **Gray**: Neutrality
- **Silver:** Connections to the moon, intuition, and reflection
- **White**: Peace, purity and purification, truth, and chastity

One very important note to keep in mind is that white is considered a valid substitute for any candle color. So, if you can't find the colored candle corresponding to your intentions, you can use a white one instead.

Choosing a Candle

There are other elements to consider when selecting a candle besides the color. The size of the candle is something else that you have to keep in mind, despite what some witches will tell you. Many spells require letting your candle burn out entirely, which means selecting one that would take four days to burn isn't exactly ideal. In this case, taper or votive candles are the best as they won't take forever to burn. However, you should also know that some spells require specific types of candles like figure or seven-day candles. In that case, look for those in local stores or online.

When preparing for a spell, never use a candle you've used for another ritual or as a light source in the bathroom or when the power goes out. You should always select new candles for your spells, not a used one that might have picked up energy from the previous usage. Another question that might pop into your head is whether you should use a scented candle. Most Wiccans prefer non-scented candles to avoid distraction.

Preparing the Candles: Cleansing and Charging

According to Wiccan tradition, you cannot buy a candle and immediately use it in a spell. It needs to be cleansed and charged first. There are different cleansing rituals and techniques, and if you have your own, that's fine. To cleanse a candle, you can rub it with sea salt or alcohol. You can also pass the candle through the smoke of sage or incense while focusing on the intention of purifying the candle in preparation for a ritual.

The next step toward preparing the candle is to anoint it, which means dressing it with oil to establish a psychic connection between you and the candle. You'd be charging the candle with your energy and intention meant for the spell so you can prepare it to burn. You can use any natural oil, but many witches go with grapeseed oil since it is odorless. You can select other essential oils with different healing qualities and correspond to certain intentions. For example, if you are about to cast a spell to banish anxiety and stress, you can use lavender oil since lavender is known to be a soother and a powerful tool to get rid of fear and anxiety.

Rub your oil, starting with the top of the candle to the middle. Then begin again from the bottom until the two layers of oil meet at the center. Some Wiccan traditions start from the middle and work the oil to the top and bottom. Some spells will require the addition of natural herbs to the spell. In that case, you can cover the anointed candle in the herbs by rolling it in the mixture you've combined. Alternatively, you can place each herb on the candle's body. Some witches charge their candle by carving a symbol or their intention onto it. This also imbues the candle with the intention of the spell but must be done before dressing it with oil.

Your Intentions Make the Spell

The most important part of candle magick is you, or rather your intentions. We mentioned earlier that you have to be clear with your intention, and I'll add "specific" as well. The clearer you are with your intentions, the more possible it is to attract that wish. You also need to be realistic with your intention and wish for something that can actually happen. For example, you can attract wealth, but wishing for something like being an astronaut and going to space is significantly less likely to happen.

I also recommend summarizing your goal in a single thought or one sentence rather than uttering a monologue or thinking about the whole scenario. If you wish to have a home, just think or say that, but don't go into the details of the house's location and the color of the fence or what kind of dog you wish to have. Before we move on from intentions, I cannot over-stress the importance of not blowing your candles. You want to snuff the candle with your finger or a dedicated tool if you can't leave it to burn out, for example, if you need to go out. If you blow the candle, you're blowing away your intentions, so let's avoid that unless you're banishing something.

By now, you understand what type of candle you need for the goal you have in mind. With your intentions clear, specific, and concise, and the candle cleansed and charged, you can begin your ritual, as I'll show you in the upcoming chapters. Whether it is love or protection, preparing your candle is the first step of the ritual.

CHAPTER 2:

CANDLE LOVE MAGICK

*"Your task is not to seek love, but merely
to seek and find all the barriers within
yourself that you have built against it."*
– Rumi

This quote is the basis on which positive love magick is based. Love spells are some of the most common in Wicca and other witchcraft movements. However, there are two types of spells to perform to attract love. The first, and the one we'll focus on, is practiced by white witches, and it doesn't change the way a person feels about you or manipulate them into falling for you. It highlights your positive qualities and helps you find the confidence to attract the kind of love you want. The other type is manipulative love spells, which aim to manipulate someone into loving you, which isn't healthy and a practice that should be avoided.

Simple Spell to Attract Love

You'll need a piece of paper and a pen, dried rose petals, cinnamon, honey, a fireproof bowl, a seven-day white candle or any white candle, and a lighter for this spell. Begin this ritual by prepa–ring your magical space, whether that's decluttering or cleansing with sage or incense. You then need to raise the positive energy within you, so do something that makes you feel good. You can put on some soothing music, dance, sing, drum, or simply go for a walk. Anoint your candle with the oil of your choice while focusing on your intentions, thus charging it.

The next step of this spell is to write down this intention on a piece of paper. Make sure you are clear and specific with your intention, which is to attract love for this spell. Fold the piece of paper into squares and make sure it's flat enough to be placed under the candle. Meditate on your intentions for a while. Put the rose petals on top of the candle with a pinch of cinnamon and a couple of teaspoons of honey. Make sure to keep them away from the wick.

Fill the bowl with water but just enough to cover the base of the candle, don't soak it. Put the piece of paper with your intentions under that bowl, and then place the candle in the water and light it. Place the bowl with the candle in it on your altar. Invoke your deities, higher self, ancestors, or whatever spirit guides you wish to bless your ritual and guide you. Ask them to help you attract love.

Meditate on your intention as the candle burns, and visualize yourself finding love and enjoying that feeling of being loved. Conjure a mental image of you attracting affection and no longer craving love because you are satisfied and fulfilled on that emotional level. Let the candle burn out completely -- or snuff it out if you have to go, but light it again when you return. When the candle has burned out completely, thank it and throw it away. Carry the piece of paper with your intentions in your wallet or hang it on your fridge.

Spell to Attract Ideal Partner

This is another candle magick spell to help create an attraction between you and someone you like. It happens quite often that we find ourselves attracted to someone that would make an ideal partner, but they might not notice you or don't necessarily think of you in the same way. This candle magick spell acts as a medium between you, helps your romantic interest see you in a different light, and highlights your qualities as a lover.

You need a pink or red candle for this spell, a red pen, white paper, and clear space for this spell. Make sure there are no distractions in your magical space. Set the mood by dimming the lights and maybe playing some soothing music. Sit before your altar and ground yourself. Take three deep breaths and focus on your breathing to calm your mind. Channel your energy into focusing on your romantic interest and how you desire to be with them. Visualize this happening and how you two would be happy together.

Light the red candle and place it on your altar. Grab the red pen and write your first name and your romantic interest's last name on the white paper. Without lifting the pen of the paper, draw two circles around both names while still focusing your intention on being together with this person. Keep visualizing the two of you ending up together. As you do that, repeat this prayer:

May our fates be intertwined
And our love forever defined

18

We are one
It is done
So, mote it be

Let the candle burn out completely, and don't blow it out. Repeat this spell for seven days in a row, and I'd recommend starting on Friday, the day of the goddess of love, Venus.

Commitment Spell

Sometimes, we find ourselves in good relationships, but they lack commitment. You can be in love with your partner, but they still have a hard time committing to you. This spell can help you strengthen your bond and give your partner the push they need to commit to the relationship fully. This is a full moon spell that aims to add more loyalty and enhance the longevity of your relationship. It's a powerful candle spell that can strengthen your ties with your partner and bind you two together.

You need a long blue or red string, two poppets to represent you and your partner, and two candles. One of them has to be red, and the other can be red or pink. While you can use clay or cloths to make the poppets, you should make it out of the wax of the red or pink candle for this full moon commitment spell. So, melt the candle and make two poppets out of its wax.

Put the red candle between the two wax poppets and wrap the three together with your string to begin the spell. Ensure the knot is tight and the candle is firmly lodged between both poppets, but don't leave a good portion of the string hanging free. When it's a full moon, light the candle and focus on your intentions of having a committed and strengthened relationship. Wrap the hanging part of the string around the poppets and the candle one more time and repeat this prayer:

> *We are bound together*
> *Committed, loving, bound*
> *And so, it shall be*

Let the candle burn for a while, and then snuff it out. Light the candle again every night for three days in a row, and on the third night, let it burn completely. Keep the remaining wax from this spell, and don't get rid of it. You can keep a healthy, committed relationship as long as you keep this wax safe.

Honey Jar Love Spell

The use of honey in spells dates back to ancient civilizations. Witches have used it for a long with love rituals, and when paired with candle magick, you can create a very powerful spell. The great thing about honey jar love spells is how diverse they are. You can use this spell to attract love, ignite a spark between you and a certain person, or rekindle the flame with an ex or an old crush. It doesn't even have to be a romantic relationship. You may want to mend a relationship with a friend or a relative and use a honey jar spell for that intention. Adding a candle to a honey jar gives you options with the spell, as I'll show you now.

Begin by writing the name of the person you wish to attract or fix a relationship with -- write it three times. Then, turn the paper by a 90-degree angle and write yours down three times as well so that the letters of both names overlap. Draw a circle around both names, and within that circle, you're going to write your intention. The most important part is not to lift your pen while writing all this down. The next part is where you focus on your intention, and it's crucial for the success of this spell. Whether you want to reconcile with a loved

21

one or ignite a flame of love, just focus on your intentions, and visualize the outcome coming to fruition. You can add the dots and cross the t's when you're done circling the names and the intentions.

Fold this paper with the names and the intention to fit inside the honey jar. Put the piece of paper inside the jar and let your fingers touch the honey. When you remove your fingers, say this prayer:

> As sweet as this honey is, so shall my connection with ___ be.

When you say the prayer, lick your fingers and close the jar. Then, you will use candle magick to set your intentions onto the universe and transform your relationship with this person. You need to select a candle beforehand suited for your intentions. Choose red if you want someone to fall for you or if you want to strengthen a bond between you and your partner, or pink if you want to highlight the nonromantic love between you and someone. You could also just use a white candle as it is neutral and can be used with any intention.

Place the candle on top of the honey jar with the folded paper and light it. Let this candle burn down until it's finished, and focus on your intentions as it does. Meditate and visualize this honey jar candle spell attracting the love and happiness you deserve. When the candle is burned out completely, don't discard it but store it in a place that only you know. After seven full days, repeat this ritual, and keep doing it on the same day, once every week, until your intentions come to fruition.

Candle Magick to Banish a Toxic Ex

This spell is a bit different from the previous few. It's not to attract love but to move from it. People can easily find themselves trapped in a toxic relationship with an abusive partner, and moving on from your feelings toward them is never easy. This powerful candle ritual will help you banish a toxic ex from your life and move on.

You need a black candle, a fireproof bowl, white sage, Florida water, scissors, and black cotton threads or yarn (prepare several yards). Start the ritual by cleansing your magical space of any lingering negative energy. Open the windows and light some incense or sage. Spray some Florida water in the corners of your room to create a safe and sacred circle. Sit before your altar and ground yourself. You can meditate to clear your thoughts. When you feel ready, light the candle, and focus on your intentions of banishing this toxic ex from your life. Visualize yourself free of loving them and no longer held back by those feelings. Focus on this intention while setting your gaze on the black candle.

Bind your feet together with the thread and say this:

> *This thread is holding me back and stopping me from moving forward.*

Next, tie your hands together and say:

> *These bonds are stopping me from receiving love.*

Meditate again and focus on the negative experience you've had with this ex and how you wish to be free of it. Let the threads around your hands and feet absorb this energy. When you're ready, cut the threads with the scissors and be careful not to harm yourself. As you cut the threads laced with negativity, say:

> *I banish __ from my life, and I release my ties to them.*
> *I am whole again, and I shall move forward.*

Burn the threads in the flame of the black candle, and toss them in the fireproof bowl. Get rid of the ashes of the threads and bury them in the ground somewhere far from your home. Let the candle burn down completely and visualize the healthier and happier version of yourself with that ex no longer part of your life.

Whether you wish to attract love or banish a toxic relationship, these candle spells can help you manifest that intention. You just need to believe that these rituals will work and let yourself be filled with positive energy to make them work. As you can see from this section, candle magick can be very powerful if paired with rituals and other practices, and you can use it to attract love and even heal from physical and emotional pain, as you'll see in this upcoming chapter.

CHAPTER 3:

CANDLE MAGIC
SPELLS FOR HEALING

"The wound is the place where the Light enters you."
— Rumi

Sometimes, toxic relationships and feelings of loneliness from not having love in our lives can leave us emotionally scarred. Some relationships can even leave you physically scared. This is why I've chosen to add candle spells to help you heal from these wounds. What's worse is not knowing what ails you. In a few cases, doctors can't find the answer and are flabbergasted about why you are in pain. We'll also explore some spells to help treat unknown pains. Remember, however, that these spells are not a substitute for seeking medical care. They can, however, complement the remedies given to you by doctors.

Pain Healing Spell

This ritual should be performed over two days, Saturday and Sunday, or entirely on a Sunday. It's a healing spell to help you regenerate from an emotional or physical injury. There are no specific ingredients for this spell. You can include herbs, natural crystals/stones, and essential oils that have a soothing effect on you and are blessed with regenerative qualities. However, you will need a candle corresponding to your intention: dark blue for emotional healing, brown for physical healing, or white.

Begin this ritual by casting your magical circle. You need to create a space where you are safe and can heal. You can make the circle out of natural stones with healing properties like quartz or amethyst. You can also make an invisible circle using an athame or your finger. Make the circle in a clockwise direction, with you in it, and visualize that it is made of protective light that can shield and heal you.

The first part of this ritual is about releasing what pains you. This means that you first need to acknowledge the injury or the trauma that left you emotionally or physically scarred. You can journal about it or focus on what happened so you can move on. Write down whatever happened that left you in need of healing. Breathe in and out slowly as you think about what happened. Then, rip the pages out of your journal and shred them. Imagine that the pain is leaving your body, and the tension is fading as you do so.

Anoint the candle with essential oils and herbs that have a special place in your heart, then light it. Light the candle and focus on its flame. Let its healing light wash over you and fill you with light that will heal your scars. Take in that healing energy coming from the candle and meditate on your intention. Conjure a mental image of a healthier you that is no longer suffering from the pain of a past injury or trauma. Let that light wrap around every fiber of your being and replace the negative energy you have released earlier onto the paper. As you focus on the flame of the candle, say this prayer:

> *By the light of this candle*
> *My wounds will heal*
> *This healing flame will wash away my pain*
> *And it shall never return again*
> *So, mote it be*

Perform this spell once every week until the candle is spent.

Healing Disease Ritual

This particular ritual is very important right now, as the world faces a global pandemic. It offers healing and protection for you and your loved ones from disease and sickness. Prepare your magical space as you normally would and cleanse the room first with sage or incense. Charge the magical space with the intention of healing from sickness and pain.

You need three candles, green, blue, and white, and a holder for each. You'll need an essential oil to anoint your candles or a mixture. You can make a mixture of rosemary, lavender, eucalyptus, and cedarwood oils, all powerful elements with healing and protective qualities. Prepare an athame or a pin, a piece of paper or a leaf from the earth, and a pen. If you can find gold ink, that'd be great. If not, use any pen.

To start the ritual, cast your magical circle and invoke whichever deities you ask for guidance during your rituals. Raise your energy by chanting or dancing. Take deep breaths to calm and center yourself if you want. Whatever you usually do to prepare for spells, do it. When you feel ready, use the pin or athame to carve the word 'protect' on the white candle, or you can carve a symbol associated with healing for you. Anoint the candle with the essential oil mixture and/or any herbs you associate with protection. Hold it in your hand and visualize a white light spreading out of the candle, engulfing and shielding you, your home, and your loved ones from pain and sickness. Light the candle and say a protective chant:

> By the flames of this candle, I am protected.
> I am safe from illness and disease.
> This white light shields my loved ones and me.
> So, mote it be.

Then, carve 'heal' on the blue candle and anoint it with essential oils and herbs you associate with healing or the same mixture you used with the one above. Hold the candle in your hand and visualize it glowing in a blue light that will grow and engulf you. It will heal your body and that of loved ones and remove any sickness. Let that soothing and restorative energy fill you up. Light the blue candle and say:

> By the flames of this blue candle, I am healed.
> This healing light surrounds us and grants us recovery and good health.
> We are whole; we are healed; we are healthy. So, mote it be.

This last part of the spell prevents the sickness from returning to your body or someone you care about. Grab the green candle and carve "security" on it. Anoint it with oils and place healing herbs on it. Hold the candle and visualize a green light spreading out of it to engulf you and your house with everyone in it. This green light is a security blanket, keeping you and your loved ones safe and securing you from ever contracting that sickness again. Light the candle and say:

By the flames of this green candle, the disease is gone and shall never return.
We are secured, prospering, and comforted, and so it shall be.

Write down these intentions for protection, healing, and security on the piece of paper. Fold it twice and seal it with some melted wax from the white candle. Keep this paper on your altar or by your bed to keep your intentions of health and security alive. Let the three candles burn out over three days.

Spell to Banish Depression

This candle healing spell is used to banish depression, anxiety, or other mental/emotional ailments. With the power of your intentions, you will charge ritual candles with your energy and desire to heal from depression. As always, remember that this spell is not a substitute for seeking medical help.

You need a blue candle for this spell, an athame/ pin, incense, a piece of paper and a pen, a healing crystal (selenite), essential oils, and some healing herbs like rosemary and lavender. Prepare for the ritual by cleansing your magical space and then casting your circle. Sit before your altar and center yourself. Begin by carving your intention on the blue candle using the athame or pin. Be specific about what you wish to heal and release, and focus on that intention in your head. You can write something along the lines of "Banish depression" or "Become happier and banish anxiety."

Next, anoint the candle with essential oils of your choosing -- go for essential oils with healing properties like sandalwood, eucalyptus, and peppermint. Charge this candle with your intention of banishing depression and becoming free of its shackles. Keep focusing on your intention as you anoint the candle, and then add the herbs. Roll it in a mixture of rosemary, lavender, garden sage, and peppermint that you've grounded earlier. The herbs will stick to the candle now that it has been anointed with the oil.

After consecrating the candle, grab the pen and paper and write down your intention on it. You can write your name as well. It's something like this: *I __ thus banish depression and anxiety from my life.* When you're done writing what you wish to banish, fold the paper, and put it on the altar. Place your blue candle over it. Grab the selenite crystal and visualize it absorbing the negativity from your body. Channel all the negative thoughts and bad feelings you've ever had into the stone and let it drain your body of the fear and the sadness.

Holding the crystal in one hand, light the blue candle with the other. Focus on the candle's flame and imagine that your depression is fading away just like the candle's smoke. Keep meditating on your intention as the candle burns, with the healing crystal in your hand, until the candle burns out completely.

Using these spells, you can invoke the help of your ancestors or deities and the universe to heal from emotional and physical pain. Don't cast these spells if you're in a bad headspace, and make sure you are filled with positive energy as you perform these healing rituals. After learning how to cast a candle healing spell, I will show you how to cast protection spells in this upcoming chapter. Peace of mind and enlightenment can be achieved, but they must be protected from the darkness surrounding us.

CHAPTER 4:

CANDLE MAGIC SPELLS FOR PROTECTION

"Goodness is sparked by a caution for the sake of what is good, not a fear of what is bad."
– Criss Jami

Witchcraft does not preach fear. It doesn't tell us to always be on guard of the evil forces at work around us and the negative energies we have to be mindful of. Witchcraft does, however, preach protecting what you love. There is much good in your life, even if you don't always see it. This is why it is your responsibility as a witch with the power to take action to protect that good. These spells I will outline will help you protect yourself, your household, and your loved ones from any darkness that may seek to harm them.

Simple Protection Spell

This spell is simple, and any witch can cast it to protect her physical and spiritual self. You need a black candle, black salt, white sage, star anise, protective crystals like black tourmaline or amethyst, a fireproof bowl, rosemary, essential oils, and mortar & pestle. Cleanse your magical space using sage or incense, or however you usually do it. I'd recommend using the black salt to cast your circle for this spell as, within it, you'd be safe from any negative energy or ill intentions. You can also place four protective crystals in each quarter of your circle to amplify its protection.

Begin heating your essential oils in the fireproof bowl or a diffuser if you have one. Place the oil inside your circle and start mixing your herbs together. Use the mortar & pestle to mix the star anise, rosemary, and white sage. Add this herbal mixture to the oil and focus on your intention. Visualize yourself being shielded from any harm that may befall you or your loved ones. Light the black candle on your altar and set your gaze on its flame while still focusing on that intention to summon a protective shield. As you do that, repeat this chant:

By the flame of this black candle
And the power of these herbs and oils and crystals
I ask for protection from all harm
That may befall me or my own
May the goddess shield me and help me remain strong
I am safe from negativity and everything that is wrong
So, mote it be

Let the candle burn out completely while meditating and focusing on your protection. You can keep one or two of the crystals with you as a symbol of the protection you're not blessed with.

Home Protection Spell

Some practices are dedicated to protecting your home, like hanging protective herbs or crystals or an iron horseshoe to prevent negative energies and ill intentions from entering your space. This spell is a more potent approach to protect your home from negative vibrations and energies that might seep through to your home and affect everyone in it.

You need a small black candle, an athame or pin, dried sage (or sage oil), a rosemary stick (rosemary oil is fine, too), and two fireproof bowls. Cleanse your tools and your home before you begin this ritual. Take the black candle and carve a protective symbol or sigil on it using the athame or pin. Protective symbols include the Eye of Horus, Solar Cross, Hamsa, Triquetra, and the Bindrune. Look each of those up if you're unsure of how to draw them. If you're using oils instead of dried herbs, anoint the candle with them. If not, place the herbs on the candle, but leave some aside.

This ritual requires that you sit before your front door, so you can temporarily move your altar there for this spell. If that space is not available, you can perform it anywhere. Put both fireproof bowls in front of you with the candle in one. Place the protective herbs in the other bowl. You can use two candles in this spell; if that is the case, you'll put an anointed candle in each bowl. Calm your mind and breathe in and out slowly, focusing on your breathing. Whether it's a candle or herbal mixture or two candles, light whatever is in both bowls.

Let the scent of the anointed candles or the herbal mixture burn and fill your house with cleansing and protective energy. Focus on the candle's flame and let it fill you with positive energy, replacing any lingering negative thoughts you might have carried into your home. Like fire transforms all, so will the flames of the candle transform any negative energy in your home into love and peace. In this focused, meditative state of mind, repeat this chant:

> *I call on rosemary and sage to impart protection upon my abode and those in it*
> *Protect and cleanse my home*
> *May the candle flame transform negativity into pure energy*
> *And ill intentions toward me into love and light and joy*
> *So, mote it be*

When you feel ready, open your front door, release the smoke of the candle and/or herbs, and visualize it carrying any negative energy along. Let the candle burn down completely. You can carry them and walk around the house to cleanse every room and then bury their remains far from your home.

Protection Spell Against Negative and Hateful People

This spell is a bit more specific as it aims to block any negative energy coming your way from harmful people. It can shield you from their ill intentions and ward off any curses or hate coming your way. For this spell, the ingredients you need are seven needles, a small bottle with a cork, rosemary, and a black candle.

As always, cleanse the room and the tools you'll use before beginning. Then, place the rosemary in the bottle while focusing your intention on blocking negative energy and hatred from affecting you and the people you care about. Visualize this destructive energy being channeled into the needles, after which the rosemary will contain it. Light the black candle and focus on its flame that acts as a powerful shield against hatred and negativity.

Start adding the needles one by one into the small bottle, and as you do that, say aloud what each needle represents. The needles are hatred, negatevety, hexes, curses, jealousy, and other ill intentions that may be aimed at you. With seven needles and seven intentions placed in the bottle, seal it with the cork. The rosemary will work to neutralize these negative energies and bad intentions, and the black candle will banish them. Tilt the black candle and use some of its wax to seal the cork even further. Bury the bottle somewhere far from your home, and let the banishing candle burn out completely.

Spell to Ward Off an Attack

Witches have a highly developed intuition and can often sense if and when someone cast a curse or hex on them. This candle spell is ideal for warding off such attacks. It will reverse the spell on the attacker and protect you and your loved ones. Smudge your altar and your magical items and perform a cleansing ritual on yourself to release any negative energy.

You need a small mirror that you don't need; it can be a hand mirror or any other portable one. On the window next to your bed, put the mirror with its front facing the sky. You will need to charge this mirror with your intention to reverse the curse and ward off the attack. Light a black candle to begin the ritual. Repeat this chant as you focus your gaze on the flame:

By the light of this black candle, I banish the curse that was put on me and my loved ones.
This mirror shall reverse the spell, and the negative energy that was meant for me shall be turned on the attacker.

Channel all your energy to the mirror and the candle. The candle will act as a shield to protect you from negative energy and banish evil intentions, while the mirror will reverse any harmful spell that might have been cast with you as the target. Visualize the hex or the curse and negative energy meant for you bouncing off the mirror toward the person who targeted you. Sit by the window and let the candle burn out as you meditate on your intention.

These candle spells can provide you with protection against the negative energy we encounter daily. You might not think that it affects you, but it does. Negative energy seeping into your home can affect your relationships with your loved ones as well as your peace of mind, so you need this kind of protection. Next, we will discuss how to invite abundance into your life now that you're in a good place physically, mentally, and spiritually.

CHAPTER 5:

CANDLE MAGIC SPELLS FOR ABUNDANCE

"When you are grateful, fear disappears,
and abundance appears."
— Anthony Robbins

Gratitude brings more abundance into your life, but practicing gratitude isn't always easy. It's a bit of a dilemma for many people as they can't practice gratitude without abundance, and they can't attract abundance without being grateful. This is where candle magick comes in. I will show you some spells to embrace the good fortune in your life and attract more abundance and joy.

Spell to Attract Abundance

Contrary to popular belief, abundance isn't just money. Abundance is happiness and wealth and the richness that can only fill your life if you're truly grateful. This candle spell can bring you luck, happiness, wealth, gratitude, and much more. I recommend doing this ritual for several days or weeks in a row, starting on the new moon, which marks new beginnings and attracts good fortune.

Make sure your magical space is cleansed and that you're comfortable and in a good mood. Whatever you usually do to charge yourself with positive energy, do it. Dance, sing, drum, play music, take a ritual bath, read, or just put on your favorite outfit. Prepare a green candle for this ritual and place a crystal for abundance on your altar like citrine. When you feel ready, grounded, and calm, sit before your altar and hold the candle in your hand. Meditate on the things you have in your life that you're grateful for. It doesn't have to be something as significant as wealth or marriage. It can be something you did to help someone or a hobby you have. There are always things to be grateful for, and you need to think about those for a while.

Abundance is gratitude for the things you are blessed with, and it's also attracting more. You need that balance, and you have to visualize it in your head because without gratitude and the desire to attract more, you can't attract abundance. Light the candle and place it on your altar. Then, declare your intentions aloud. What kind of abundance do you wish to attract? Is it wealth? Gratitude? Joy? How would that feel, and why do you want it? Don't hold back and ask the universe for your heart's deepest desires, and release this positive energy into the candle. Picture these positive wishes fueling the candle's flame and whisper it all to the fire. Make sure you're close to the candle but be careful not to get burned.

After speaking your intentions, close your eyes, meditate on these wishes and let yourself fill with positive energy. Let the candle burn, and grab your journal. Write down what abundance means in your life and why you wish to attract it, or write personal affirmations. This is one of those few rituals where you should blow the candle to release your intentions into the universe. Take the citrine stone off your altar and carry it in your pocket.

Spell to Attract Prosperity and Abundance

This is another prosperity and abundance spell that can be used to attract wealth and money or whatever you wish to be abundant in your life. You need a small green candle, a coin, fireproof bowl, an athame or pin, square green cloth, pure vanilla or vanilla bean, and powdered cinnamon or pure Ceylon cinnamon oil. This spell should be performed on a waxing moon to charge it with lunar power and attract abundance.

Carve a prosperity symbol on the green candle with the pin or athame like the number '3,' which corresponds to abundance and good fortune. You can also write down words like wealth, joy, abundance, or prosperity instead. Consecrate the candle with the cinnamon and vanilla, and recite this prayer: *I call on these magic herbs to unleash my potential. May they attract prosperity and good fortune into my life. Money, joy, and abundance come to me, so mote it be.*

Place the coin in the fireproof bowl and the candle on top of it. Light the candle and focus on your intentions. Visualize yourself turning around and prosperity filling it. Let these positive feelings wash over you. Let the green candle burn down entirely, then take the coin from underneath the wax and wrap it in the green cloth. Carry it in your wallet or your pocket wherever you go. Get rid of any remaining wax far from your home; bury it if you can.

Spell to Attract Money

While the spells above were for abundance and could implicitly include money, this one is specifically for attracting money. It's a simple ritual to bring more money into your life. You could add more ingredients if you wish, but you only need a green candle to try this spell out. You don't need to be in debt to perform this ritual, as its purpose is to attract wealth regardless of your current financials.

To cast this spell, you need to raise your energy more than you usually do at the beginning of a ritual. So, perform an energetic activity like chanting, dancing, or drumming. Make some noise and create positive energy within you. Sit before your altar and consecrate the candle when you feel comfortable and positive enough. Use essential oils and/or herbs you feel comfortable with and are associated with abundance like rosemary, basil, dandelion, and calendula. Carve your name on the candle using a pin or athame.

Light the candle and place it on the altar. Stare into the flame and let your mind drift away into a deep meditative state. Close your eyes and begin to visualize money flowing into your life, and you buy all the things you want with it. Let that positive feeling of wealth fill you up, and make sure the money and the things you'll do with it are real in your head. As you visualize this, repeat this prayer three times:

> *Wealth, money, and fortune flow into my life*
> *In no means that harm or pain another*
> *Fill my life with joy and prosperity*
> *May wealth find me in perpetuity*
> *So, mote it be*

Light the green candle every day while repeating this chant three times every night until it burns out. Don't throw it away. Retain it and wait for the money to flow into your life as you have wished for.

CHAPTER 6:

CANDLE MAGIC SPELLS FOR EMPLOYMENT

"Joblessness is a time for reflection"
— Sunday Adelaja

Everyone struggles with their professional lives at some point, but that is no reason to despair. With enough luck and hard work and these spells, you can attract any job, even your dream one. Cast these spells when you are facing trouble on the job front, whether you've been unemployed for a while or stuck in a hopeless job that you don't like.

Spell for Good Luck with Job Hunting

Candle magick is very powerful and effective for those looking for help with employment in general. You can change the color of the candle depending on the purpose of your spell. For this one, you want confidence and good fortune while you're job hunting, so get a yellow or gold candle. You'll also need olive oil and matches or a lighter.

Put the candle on the altar and make sure you've prepared the space for the spell. Anoint it with olive oil or use other essential oils that have a special meaning for you. Charge the candle with your intentions, and make sure you transfer only positive energy into it. Light the gold or yellow candle and repeat this prayer three times:

> *For me, a good job awaits*
> *By the blessing of this bright light*
> *And the power of this flame*
> *There is a place for me*
> *And a good job awaits me*
> *I have faith that the universe will help me*
> *So, mote it be*

Repeat this three times, and let the candle burn for nine minutes while focusing on your intention and visualizing yourself getting a job offer. Draw a mental image of yourself enjoying your new job and finding good fortune on the employment front. Then, snuff out the flame and repeat this ritual once every Sunday until you get that job offer you've been waiting for or the candle is spent. If by then you haven't received the job offer, get a new candle, and repeat the ritual every Sunday until you do.

Career Success Spell

Sometimes, it's about keeping and protecting your job rather than finding one, and this spell helps you do that. This ritual can give you a much-needed boost in your professional life. You'll need some essential oils: rosemary, cinnamon, and ginger, four candles; white, green, red, and yellow, and a candle snuff. Prepare a piece of paper and a pen.

Cleanse your energy however you usually do, but I'd recommend taking a ritual bath with some rosemary oil or leaves. When you feel refreshed and ready, go to your altar, and write down what you wish to attract to your career. It can be protecting your job or getting a promotion or a raise. Try to be specific about your intentions and write down what kind of career success you hope to attract. Let the intentions flow out of you and into the paper.

Next, anoint each candle with a drop of each of the essential oils you've prepared. Ginger will attract good fortune and bless your career, cinnamon will attract money, and rosemary will banish negative energy and misfortune as well as any blockages that might be stopping you from manifesting your goals. Place the four candles around the piece of paper with your intentions and light them. The green candle will attract wealth and abundance, the white one will dispel negative energy, the red candle will give you courage and power to accomplish your goals, and the yellow one will boost your confidence and help you achieve your goals.

With the four candles lit, close your eyes and relax. Sink into a deep meditative state where you can visualize these intentions coming to life. Picture a more successful and accomplished version of yourself and take control of your destiny. Meditate for a few minutes and repeat a chant:

> *By the power of these candles, I ask for guidance and aid.*
> *May the universe bless my career, and these flames bring me fortune and good luck.*

Snuff out your candles and repeat this candle ritual for six days in a row, and on the seventh day, let each candle burn out completely. Keep the paper with your intentions and aspirations with you until you achieve what was written in it. Once you do, burn the paper, and thank the universe for manifesting your goals.

CONCLUSION

"No one saves us but ourselves. No one can, and no one may. We ourselves must walk the path."
—Gautama Buddha

In this book, I set out to show you how you can take control of your destiny. Sooner or later, we all experience some misfortune in life, but it's up to us to pick ourselves up and move on. It's up to you to surrender to the hardships of life or to take action and seize control of your destiny. Using these spells, you can attract the things you've often dreamed of and think impossible. You can also banish the negative feelings and darkness that seek to hold you back and stop you from realizing your full potential.

Candle magick is powerful magick, but it's only as powerful as you believe it to be. With enough positive energy and faith, you can manifest these dreams of yours. You can heal from past trauma and injury. You can find love and be emotionally satisfied. You can protect your house and everyone in it. You can find the job you've dreamed of for many years. With candle spells, you can fill your life with an abundance of joy and satisfaction. I added spells that are easy to apply and require minimal ingredients. The beauty of candle magick is that you can practice it and change your reality with only a candle and your own energy. You just need to start, and the spells in this book are a great place to do that. So, read these spells, find yourself some candles, and make things happen.

REFERENCES

A candle healing spell. (2021, November 2). ☽ Well Divined. https://welldivined.com/a-candle-healing-spell/

A protection spell against negative people. (2021, November 2). ☽ Well Divined. https://welldivined.com/a-protection-spell-against-negative-people/

A simple protection spell. (2021, November 2). ☽ Well Divined. https://welldivined.com/a-simple-protection-spell/

A witch's guide to cord-cutting, the simple ritual to get over your ex. (n.d.). Vice.Com. Retrieved from https://www.vice.com/en/article/mbz3na/how-to-do-cord-cutting-ritual-witch-spell-breakup

All Answers Ltd. (2021, December 31). History of candle magic. Ukessays.Com; UK Essays.

https://www.ukessays.com/essays/cultural-studies/the-history-of-candle-magick-cultural-studies-essay.php

An astrological forecast for 2022. (2021, December 30). Goop. https://goop.com/ca-en/wellness/spirituality/horoscope-predictions-2022/

Best Love Spells - Improve your relationships & experiences with others. (2021, August 13). Baltimore Magazine. https://www.baltimoremagazine.com/special/best-love-spells-improve-your-relationships-and-experiences-with-others/

Candle magic for beginners. (2017, June 29). Wiccan Spells. https://wiccanspells.info/wiccan-pagan-articles/candle-magic-for-beginners/

Comiskey, B. (2019a, March 7). Abundance spell. Tip of the Moon. https://tipofthemoon.store/spells/abundance

Comiskey, B. (2019b, June 4). Healing spell. Tip of the Moon. https://tipofthemoon.store/spells/healing-spell

Dombrowski, K. (2020, March 17). Blessing spell for protection, healing, and security in response to Covid-19 —. Kiki Dombrowski. https://www.kikidombrowski.com/blog/blessing-spell-for-protection-healing-and-security-in-response-to-covid-19

Love spells that work, best love spell caster guide. (2021, August 17). Juneau Empire. https://www.juneauempire.com/national-marketplace/love-spells-that-work-best-love-spell-caster-guide/

May, A. (2020, February 7). 9 powerful protection symbols explained. Welcome To Wicca Now. https://wiccanow.com/9-protection-symbols/

Morgan, B. (2018, October 2). You need these magical spell candles. House Beautiful. https://www.housebeautiful.com/shopping/home-accessories/g23572014/magic-spell-candles/

Pollux, A. (2019a, November 21). Our #1 career success spell for attaining your goals. Welcome To Wicca Now. https://wiccanow.com/our-career-success-spell-to-help-attain-your-goals/

Pollux, A. (2019b, November 27). An easy abundance spell using cinnamon and vanilla.

Welcome To Wicca Now.
https://wiccanow.com/an-easy-abundance-spell-using-cinnamon-and-vanilla/

Pollux, A. (2019c, November 28). Our powerful home protection spell with sage and Rosemary. Welcome To Wicca Now. https://wiccanow.com/powerful-home-protection-spell-with-sage-and-rosemary/

Smith, E. W. (2019, May 3). A beginner's guide to candle magic. Refinery29.Com; Refinery29. https://www.refinery29.com/en-us/what-is-candle-magic-meaning

The transforming power of fire - Pepi de Boissieu. (n.d.). Pepideboissieu.Com. Retrieved from https://pepideboissieu.com/The-transforming-power-of-fire

Ward, K. (2021, December 23). Your everything-you-need-to-know intro to candle magick. Cosmopolitan. https://www.cosmopolitan.com/lifestyle/a31133533/candle-magic-colors-meaning/

Wigington, P. (n.d.). How to use candle magic in spells. Learn Religions. Retrieved from https://www.learnreligions.com/introduction-to-candle-magic-2561684

Your guide to candle magic. (n.d.). Rylandpeters. Retrieved from https://rylandpeters.com/blogs/health-mind-body-and-spirit/your-guide-to-candle-magic

(N.d.). Lamag.Com. Retrieved from https://www.lamag.com/article/best-love-spells-magical-ways-to-influence-relationships-and-love